I0796345

ZONDERVAN

Getting Through What You're Going Through

Published by Zondervan, 3950 Sparks Drive SE, Suite 101, Grand Rapids, MI 49546, USA. Zondervan is a registered trademark of The Zondervan Corporation, L.L.C., a wholly owned subsidiary of HarperCollins Christian Publishing, Inc. Requests for information should be addressed to customercare@harpercollins.com.

ISBN 978-0-3104-6574-4
ISBN 978-0-3104-6576-8 (audiobook)
ISBN 978-0-3104-6573-7 (eBook)

HarperCollins Publishers, Macken House, 39/40 Mayor Street Upper, Dublin 1, D01 C9W8, Ireland (https://www.harpercollins.com)

Author is represented by The Christopher Ferebee Agency, www.christopherferebee.com.

Art direction: Tiffany Forrester
Interior design: Lori Lynch
Interior illustrations: Brad Woodard

Printed in Canada

26 27 28 29 30 MAC 6 5 4 3 2

FOR THOSE SEARCHING FOR
A SPARK OF HOPE.
FOR THOSE COURAGEOUSLY
TAKING THE NEXT STEP.
FOR THOSE WHO NEED TO REMEMBER
THAT LIFE IS STILL WORTH LIVING.
FOR THOSE HOLDING ON TO THE
PROMISE THAT GOOD IS ON THE WAY.
FOR THOSE WHO JUST NEED A MOMENT
TO BE STILL AND BREATHE.
THIS IS FOR YOU.

CONTENTS

INTRODUCTION

It was the first week of January, and I once again believed this was the year I was going to be in the best shape of my life. I started running, stretching, and working out. I even did some sit-ups.

New year, new me, right?

Not for long. Only seven days into the new year, I woke up at two a.m. in horrific pain. My lower back, abdomen, and hips were throbbing. The pain was unbearable. I wanted to throw up and cry and pass out. (Not to brag, but I didn't.)

I typed my symptoms into Google, thinking it was a muscle strain or back spasm, but according to the World Wide Web, I was either on my period or pregnant. No matter what I did the discomfort remained. I couldn't sleep or get comfortable. Ibuprofen didn't relieve the pain. The heating pad didn't change how I felt. Ice didn't work.

My wife, Sarah, finally suggested we go to the ER, where, after a CT scan and some blood work, the doctor pulled me into a small room and cleared his throat.

"Well, it looks like you've got an ulcer, Mr. Olson."

"Does this require surgery?" I asked.

"No, but it does require some lifestyle changes."

Even worse, I thought.

"What do you do for a living?" he asked.

"I'm a writer."

"Are you stressed out?"

"Yes."

"Do you drink a lot of coffee?"

"Yes."

"Do you have a hard time slowing down?"

"Yes."

I was beginning to wonder if the doctor knew anything about being a writer. The truth is, before this hospital visit, I thought I was doing just fine. My wife had been teaching me how to rest, and every week for a year I had taken a day and a half, sometimes two, off from work.

But it turns out resting does not always mean less stress.

Stress is complicated. It sneaks through the front door, bringing its friends Insecurity and Worry. They wrap their greasy little hands around my shoulders and get me to believe I must do it all. And if I don't do it all, nothing will get done—and I will no longer be a full-time writer and will become a forgotten failure.

And the last thing I want to become is a forgotten failure.

As it turns out, that is one easy way to get an ulcer.

That's how, in the cold of the emergency room on a Monday night, after answering a doctor's questions, I realized it was time for a change. So, that's what I'm doing. I'm paying attention to what I put into my body and how it affects me. Things like coffee and media and food. I'm prioritizing what needs to be prioritized. I'm creating healthy boundaries and sticking with them. I'm admitting weaknesses and reminding myself that God knows what I need. I'm saying yes to slowing down and no to the things I cannot control. I'm telling myself it isn't "On your mark, get set, go!" It's "On your mark, get set, *slow*."

Most importantly, I'm learning to trust God. My ulcer was a symptom of stress, and my stress was a symptom of pride. When the world was on my shoulders, I would forget that the love of Christ is certain and strong. I would claw and scramble and spin the tires and overthink and say yes to something I should say no to and slam another cup of coffee and keep going.

Maybe you're in a similar place. You know you need to make changes. You know the way things are now aren't the way they should be.

HOLD ON TO THE TRUTH THAT HOPE IS NOT DISTANT.

Remind yourself to slow down, breathe deep, and remember God is faithful. Tell yourself it's okay to rest and make changes and start again.

Hold on to the truth that hope is not distant. Hope is here, guiding you as you learn to breathe again, be again, and live again.

Learn to breathe again.

Learn to be again.

Learn to live again.

I

GETTING THROUGH & GOING THROUGH

DON'T SKIP TO THE END

It's hard to sit with what is
when what is
is not what you want it to be.
But let's not skip to the end.
Sit with what is
and continue to let
the light pour in.

Some days I want to jump to the good parts.
I want to skip the line and get on the ride.
I want to hop on the highway and fly through the red lights.
Give me the chance to cut a corner, and I'll take it.
Even if I know I'll regret it.

It's hard to be where you are
when where you are
is not where you want to be.
But I have to believe there is something for us
in the here and now.

In the waiting.
In the praying.
In the trusting.

Maybe I won't see what that is until I look back.
Most days I cannot wait to look back,
but today I'll just be right where I am.
I won't try to hit fast-forward
or skip to the end.

I'll exhale and wait.
I'll look up and pray.
I'll hold fast and trust.
I'll sit with what is
because even in this
the light is pouring in.

PEP TALK

Lighten up.
You don't need to take with you all that you're carrying.
Sort through the cracks and corners and drawers of
    your life.
Let go of what you need to let go of.
Give away what you need to give away.
Hold on to what you need to hold on to.

Stand in front of a mirror, look yourself in the eyes,
    and tell yourself what is true:
It's going to be alright.
God is faithful.
You can start again.
Grace is for you.
You're going to be okay.
You're here.
You're alive.
Lighten up.

JUST GET THROUGH IT

We sat around a campfire a half hour outside of Orlando—me and about twenty high school students. We were in the shadow of Mickey Mouse's left ear as the logs crackled, sending sparks into the sky like a fireworks show for ants. As the southern wind moved the smoke over, around, and into us, seeping into our clothes, I did what I have done for years: I stood in front of a group of strangers to share some hope.

Earlier that day, a friend had asked if I would talk with a group of high school leaders from across the state, and I couldn't say no. I never miss a chance to share with the younger generation that Jesus loves them and they aren't alone, a burden, or forgotten. When I tell them those things, I am also reminding myself that Jesus loves me and I am not alone, a burden, or forgotten.

I am okay.

I wasn't okay in high school, but I am now.

Although it was close to fifteen years ago, it seems like yesterday I was walking the halls of Oviedo High School in Central Florida. Back then I was confused, overwhelmed, curious, and hopeful. (I still am, but with a little more experience and a few more answers to the questions I once had.)

I remember what it was like to be in high school. I remember the anxiety, the pressure, the hormones. I remember getting lost thinking about the future and struggling to stay in the present. I remember wondering if everything would be okay.

I wondered out loud, asked the students, "What's life like for y'all these days?"

Immediately a boy said what you and I tend to say.

"Busy!"

Everyone nodded.

"Tiring," said a girl.

Everyone continued to nod.

Then, under the prying eyes of The Mouse, one of the seventeen-year-old students spoke up.

"Life is heavy and challenging. My mom tells me to just get through it, so that's what I'm doing."

In the past I would have nodded in agreement with her. I once believed I just had to get through it, but I don't anymore. So I told her what I would tell my high school self.

LET JOY MEET YOU WHERE YOU ARE.

"I know life is a lot right now. I can't imagine getting through what you are going through. But with the fifteen years I have on you, I can say this with certainty: You don't have to 'just get through it.' *Go* through it. Go through this one life with an open hand and an open heart. As you go, stay curious, kind, and hopeful. Let joy meet you where you are. Breathe in deep and hold on tight to the miracle of this life—to be here and alive. Go through this life with tears, questions, and sleepless nights. With friends, family, and friends who have become family. With hope, love, and faith. Whatever you do, go through it. Go through it *all*."

A silence settled as I wondered if I had said too much. I always wonder if I've said too much. I looked up from the fire to see all of them nodding.

"Yeah?" I asked.

They continued nodding.

"Maybe we should just eat a s'more?"

They continued nodding.

YOU CANNOT MAKE GOD HURRY

You cannot make God hurry.

He holds time in His hands
and His timing is perfect,
but according to my watch,
He's late.

The life I have isn't half bad,
but I am far from feeling whole,
like there is a chip or crack somewhere in my soul.

Dreams are disappearing as my reality is being reshaped.
Grief and shame have found their ways into the center frame.
Breaks in my foundation
have made me long for something new.
I know something more is happening than I can see,
but what I see is life slipping away from me.

I can't be the only one who feels this way.

I can't be the only one who's tossing and turning at night,
wondering if everything will be alright,
asking God questions beginning with *when* and *why*.
I can't be the only one who's tired of feeling stuck or behind,
like I'm standing in the wrong line.

But I also know God is never far off.
He's in the waiting.
He's in the wondering.
He's before me and behind.
He's in the here and now,
just like He will be in the there and then.

God is merciful and gracious,
slow to anger and abounding in steadfast love and faithfulness.
He does things differently.
He does not punish or push us away.
He stays right here, inviting us to trust and wait.
You cannot make God hurry,
but you can join Him in the certain and slow.
And God is slow, until He isn't.

I AM WHERE I AM

Sometimes I feel like
everyone and everything
are moving and growing,
and I am just
here.

But I am still believing and trusting and trying.

I am where I am.

I can only be where I am.

And one day,
when I look back,
I'll see something more was happening all along.

ALWAYS HOPE

AS YOU WAIT, TRUST.

AS YOU TRUST, REMEMBER.

AS YOU REMEMBER, REJOICE.

AS YOU REJOICE, BREATHE.

AS YOU BREATHE, CONTINUE.

AS YOU CONTINUE, HOPE.

ALWAYS HOPE.

A Recipe to Cure Another Defeating Day

Serves 1

1/2 bag of jalapeño chips
Psalm 23
73 dog videos
A prayer
41 minutes of walking outside beneath the sun
A list of 25 things that bring you joy
10 hours in sweatpants
Another prayer
At least 2 pages of journaling
A mountain of blankets
3 hours of petting a dog
As many phone calls with old friends as desired
2 mixtapes from high school so you can sing at the top of your lungs as you drive with the windows down
A meaningful hug
Season 4, episode 13, of *The Office*
Something fried and dipped in sauce
Another prayer

1. Mix ingredients together in any order.
2. The phone calls are optional, but the prayers are not.
3. Remember today is today, and tomorrow is on its way.

OVER-EASY

Before I fell asleep last night, I began thinking about breakfast. Some people think about what they are going to wear the next day. I think about what I'm going to eat.

I decided on an over-easy egg and toast with too much butter. (I married a girl from the Midwest, and these people know how to do butter. I thought Southerners knew how to do butter, but I was wrong. Think of the normal amount of butter for a piece of toast and then triple it. They don't mess around.)

Every few months or so, my stomach and brain and heart have a three-way call to discuss if it's time to change what we are having for breakfast. Recently I had been on a yogurt and granola kick, but they voted it was time to return to eggs and toast. I wasn't upset by their unanimous decision.

In the morning, I filled the pan with butter and waited for it to dance. I grabbed one egg and cracked it perfectly in the center of the pan.

It was beautiful—white on the outside, bright yellow on the inside.

I waited patiently, watching the heat change the texture and color of the egg. When the time was right, I flipped it over and let the other side warm up, but not for too long. The yolk needs to be perfectly undercooked so once cut into, it can stretch out and run wild and free.

Is there a better bite on earth than buttered toast covered in runny yellow yolk? The small things in life are the big things. Like getting a couple of green lights on a drive home. Or a surprise text from a friend you were thinking of the day before. Or a stranger complimenting your outfit but not in a weird way. Small things can make or break everything.

SMALL THINGS CAN MAKE OR BREAK EVERYTHING.

I grabbed the spatula and stepped up to the sizzling pan.

"Don't ruin this," I told myself in the quiet of the kitchen. I slowly nestled the spatula beneath the white outside and yellow inside, careful not to disrupt the shape of the egg. My hand shaking, I gently lifted the egg and began to flip it. And then . . . the egg didn't flip. It flopped. Yolk splattered and oozed all over the pan. My perfect egg ruined. A complete disaster.

This is not how today was supposed to begin. Maybe tomorrow I'll have the perfect bite of buttered toast covered in runny yellow yolk.

Lord, in Your mercy, hear my prayer.

ALWAYS MORE IN THE BACK

I find myself torn between where I am
    and where I want to be.
Caught thinking about what I want, what I don't have,
    and what I need.
Deep down, I believe this life isn't about me,
    but I can't stop my mind from looking inside.

I take a minute to step back and see,
through the noise and silence,
heavy and light,
God has set a table and fed me day and night.

He's cared for my every need, pulled the weeds,
    planted and watered the seeds.
Like with the two fish and five loaves of bread,
    He's taken a little and cared abundantly for me.
He's topped off my cup with a generous pour,
    proving He always has more.
Time and time again God has shown me His goodness,
    that out of the emptiness, He fills.

So, I'll sit here, with hands open, and slow my anxious mind
as I remember what a friend once said:

In Him I have all I need, there is nothing I lack.
God is a gracious host, there is always more in the back.[1]

BEFORE YOU GET UP & GO

Find a moment of rest.
Begin with remembering grace.
It's for you.
Hold tight the promise of peace.
It's with you.
Remember you are not what you achieve.
You are worthy because you are worthy.
Open your hands and trust that every need has been met
and every prayer heard and every sin forgiven.
Remind yourself that even in this you can rest
and trust and hope and continue.
And you are not continuing alone.
You are being led forward by the steady hand of Mercy.

I HATE THIS FOR YOU

When someone shares with me a struggle or concern, I feel pressured to say the right thing at the right time and in the right way.

As good as my intentions are, in the moment, if I am being honest, I hardly ever get my response correct. I fumble over my words and offer something I end up wanting to take back. I suggest a book to read or a podcast to listen to or compare their struggle to someone else's. In a time of vulnerability, these things are hardly helpful. Hours later a light bulb goes off above my head, and I realize what I should have said. Usually, it's too late.

The other day I was on the other side of the conversation. I was sharing with a friend something that had been troubling me. They listened patiently. They nodded along. They didn't interrupt or change the subject.

I FELT SEEN. I FELT KNOWN.

Then, after a moment or two of silence, they said exactly what I needed to hear: "I hate this for you."

I didn't need them to send me Jeremiah 29:11. I didn't need them to respond with "It could be worse." (No one *ever* needs you to respond with "It could be worse.") I didn't need them to say sorry for something that wasn't their fault. I didn't need them to remind me God's timing is perfect. I didn't need them to share a story about how they had a friend going through something similar. I didn't need them to tell me it would get better.

I needed to hear them say, "I hate this for you."

Their response didn't bring healing or make me magically feel better, but it did make me feel less alone. I felt seen. I felt known.

Because I hated this for me too.

WE KEEP WALKING BY FAITH

I do not know what else to tell you other than we keep
walking by faith.
There are no "5 Steps to an Easier Life" or
"3 Ways to Become Better at Living."
You won't be able to find a shortcut or skip ahead.
All we can do is take one step at a time as we keep trusting.
We step into the unknown with our hands open.
We stumble and fall and are picked back up again and
again.
We look for miracles in the mundane.
We hold on to hope with tired hands.
We wrestle with the heaviness of life.
We are carried through disappointment.
We savor seasons of joy.
We find peace in the presence of God.
We suffer.
We pray.
We grieve.
We question.
We wait.
We celebrate.
We rest.
We go.

We sin.

We confess.

We receive grace upon grace upon grace.

Our cups are never empty, and our hope is never lost.

We look back and see goodness and mercy have been following us all our days.

We look ahead and see how everything is certain and unknown.

We remember the tomb is empty and Christ is alive.

We plant our lives in the garden of God's hands and pray for rain.

We keep our eyes on heaven and remember this is not the way it will always be.

We are not delusional, just like we are not forgotten.

We are hopeful.

We are trusting. I do not know what else to tell you, but carry on.

Keep walking by faith.

I DON'T KNOW

I DON'T KNOW WHAT IS AHEAD,
BUT I'VE LIVED THROUGH WHAT IS BEHIND,
AND SOMEHOW, SOME WAY,
HERE I STAND ALIVE.

THE OTHER SIDE OF THIS

Someday you'll be on the other side of this.
You'll have new ground under your feet
    and a different view in front of you,
    but the same hope burning inside your chest.
Behind will be what was, and you'll wonder
    how you made it through,
    but you made it through.

Someday, and maybe even today, you'll marvel at the kindness of God.
How He can bring you through to the other side.
How He can give a new song to old lungs.
How He can turn dead ends into beautiful beginnings.

Keep going, and let your hope continue to burn.
And someday you'll once again be on the other side of this.

NO, EVERYTHING IS NOT AS IT SHOULD BE

No, everything is not as it should be.

I know this because my favorite team has yet to win a championship. My memaw passed before I was tall enough to grab one of her cookies off the kitchen counter. My front left tire leaks air, our kitchen table wobbles, and the back deck is beginning to slowly fall apart.

Everything feels like it's slowly falling apart.

My knees crack when I stand, and my back is tight, and my blood pressure is not ideal. Wars continue. Children are starving. Families are fighting. The elderly are being forgotten. Dreams are disappearing. Everyone is addicted to their phones. The Arctic is melting. Tigers are nearing extinction. The ocean is full of garbage. Division is causing ripples, and we are getting washed away.

And I think I am allergic to gluten.

No, everything is not as it should be.

Not yet.

HOW TO MAKE IT FROM MONDAY TO FRIDAY

To get from Monday to Friday, you'll have to get out of bed five times.
Some weeks this will seem like a lot, but most good gifts can feel overwhelming at first.

To make it to the weekend, you'll need to do things to keep you going:
Get outside.
Take a break from screens.
Hold fast to the truth.
Eat chocolate of any kind: brownies, chocolate chip cookies, hot chocolate, cake, Reese's Peanut Butter Cups (or if you're fancy, you can get the dark chocolate peanut butter cups from Trader Joe's, but I am warning you, you'll get addicted).
Make plans so you can have something to look forward to.
Leave your phone in the other room, but be sure to call your mom or dad or sibling or someone who can remind you that you are loved and seen and prayed for.
Take a minute to watch videos of dogs on the internet or watch them at the park.
Let the dirty dishes pile up before you wash them down.
Scroll through Zillow and dream.

Walk the neighborhood.
Sing with the music loud and the windows down.
Order some sort of seasonal latte.
Count your blessings. Count them again.
Give yourself moments of stillness and stretching and
silence.
Spend a few nights in your favorite sweatshirt.
Speak with God. Short prayers, long prayers, morning,
afternoon, and evening prayers.
Don't forget to watch the sun rest and rise.
And as the colors mix with the sky,
remind yourself that you were made to do both:
rest and rise.
Empty your hands but keep holding on to hope.
Confess your sins and go forward with grace.

To get from Monday to Friday, you'll have to get out of bed
five times.
What a gift.

YOU ARE LOVED REGARDLESS

A few months ago, my friend Gabe sent me a text out of the blue. It said something I wish he had sent years earlier:

"You are loved regardless of your performance."

I've always been quick to fall for the lie that I need to earn the love of those around me. Maybe that's why I was the class clown in school. If I was funny, they would love me. Maybe that's why I write books and perform spoken word poetry now. If I can make others feel something, I'll have made it. Funny how we get these things so wrong.

"How'd you know I needed to hear that?" I asked Gabe.

"Because I needed to hear it," he replied.

(There is no sense in keeping the things we need to hear just to ourselves.)

I AM WORTH LOVING JUST BECAUSE I AM HERE.

Somewhere deep inside me was a dark lie that I could be loved only if I did something to earn it. And the lie didn't stop with other people. I thought I had to perform for God to see me, to hear me, to love me. But it turns out God loves me simply because He loves me. I cannot earn His love.

I am worth loving just because I am here.

You wouldn't believe how long it took for me to write that sentence.

One day I hope to believe it.

HOPE ANYWAY

When the thing that was never supposed to happen happens. When you pray for change but everything remains the same. When the sun hides and storms continue to arrive. When you feel stuck or behind or lost or alone or far from home. When life hasn't gone the way you thought it would. When you don't know how you'll make it through another day. When what was going to be a season turns into a decade. When words cut deep. When joy feels out of reach. When loneliness becomes your friend. When your voice shakes. When your footing slips. When your faith is tested. When life feels heavy. When trust is broken. When trying turns up empty-handed. When comparison covers your eyes. When change leaves you exhausted. When the green light turns red and you're stopped in another season of waiting. When you feel forgotten. When you no longer recognize the person in the mirror. When you say goodbye to a loved one before you are ready to say goodbye. When you can no longer just shake it off. When one day ends and you aren't ready for another to begin. When all you can do is hope anyway.

I'M HERE. I'M ALIVE.

Put down what is in your hands.
Not forever, but for now.
And go.
Take off your shoes and step outside.
Look up.
Move your head from left to right across the sky.
Feel the wind.
Listen to the trees.
Learn from the birds.
Open your hands and let go of what you're holding so tightly.
Before you go back inside and pick up what you put down, breathe in deep.
As your body fills with air, let these words roll in the back of your mind:

I'M HERE. I'M ALIVE.

And exhale.
Breathe in deep.
And exhale.
Breathe in deep.
And exhale.
I'm here. I'm alive.

TWO TABLES DOWN

Two tables down from me are two people sitting together. They're close enough to hear but not far enough to ignore—having a conversation I've heard and had a hundred times.

Someone apologizes for being late. After a hug or two and ordering something to drink, the conversation progresses to "How are you?" No one ever tells the truth right away. This is a rule. You must wait to share how you really feel. You can't dive into the deep end first.

To begin, you need to dip your toe in.

"Good, good! How are you?"

"I'm good too!"

I AM HERE TO LISTEN AND WRITE AND EAVESDROP FROM TWO TABLES AWAY.

I want to interrupt and say that teachers and nurses do *good* and that they are doing *well,* but I am not here to correct. I am here to listen and write and eavesdrop from two tables away.

After this, they will get off topic. They *have* to get off topic. It's part of the coffee shop conversation dance. They might bring up a mutual friend or a TV show they're watching or a meme they saw while scrolling that morning. They might talk about one of the big three: weather, traffic, or work. They might discuss how good their coffee tastes or how cute the coffee shop is or whether that guy two tables down is listening to their conversation.

He is.

After a while they will come back to where they started.

"So," one will say as they lean in, "how are you *really*?"

The word *really* changes everything. It really does. This is the question both have been wanting to ask and be asked, but it takes some time to get there.

And this morning, two tables over, I hear the other one say what I have heard and said a hundred times myself. Slowly and with long pauses, she answers truthfully.

"I don't know. I just don't feel like me. When I look at everyone else, I feel like I've gone wrong. This isn't where I thought I would be at this point in my life. Life wasn't supposed to turn out this way." She breaks eye contact, and her shoulders drop.

Empathy exudes from across the table. "I get that. I feel it too."

In the silence that follows, I stop listening and start to write.

I feel it too.

THE WAY LIFE IS

On the days when you find yourself
where you never thought you would be,
escape the noise, join the stillness,
and maybe you'll begin to see.
Step outside with empty hands.
Bring nothing with you as you leave your distractions
behind and find some space
in the wilderness of this life.

Be alone and be there.
Rest and be.
This is courageous work.
Admire the trees and listen to the birds sing.
Sit beside the water and breathe in deep.
Clear your mind and come alive.

When you are ready, tell God.
Speak out loud and uncover the words buried deep inside,
the words you think no one wants to hear.
He wants to hear from you.

Open your hands and let go.

Flex your fingers and feel the weight of nothing as you are
surrounded by everything.
Hold still as you remember the way life is right now is not
the way it will always be.

Change takes time.
You are slowly becoming and changing like the sky above
and the world around.

You cannot slow down time or speed up growth,
but you can learn the song of life,
the rhythm and flow, and dance with it
through the seasons and silence and storms,
the steps forward and back,
the waves of grief and moments of joy,
the questions and answers, the wanting and wondering.

You can let today be the first day of a new chapter.
You can let go of what's keeping you from coming alive.
You can begin again with grace and trust you are free.

When you find yourself where you never thought
you would be, join the stillness
and you'll see the way life is right now
is not the way it will always be.

TODAY

THE BEST THING
I CAN DO TODAY
BEGINS AND ENDS
WITH SLOWING DOWN
AND SAYING AMEN.

CONTINUE ALONG THE PATH

Continue along the path.
Leave your belongings behind.
One small step in front of the other.
Head up, eyes ahead, hands open.

Continue along the path.
Even if some say turn around.
Even without knowing what's ahead.
Even when the light fades to night and the sun is traded for a storm.

Continue along the path.
Forward is the way.
Slow is the pace.
God is the guide.

Continue along the path.
With peace.
With trust.
With hope.
With grace.
With love.

Continue along the path.
Be amazed.
Be changed.
Be present.

Continue along the path.
Goodness follows.
Mercy is ahead.
And the One who has invited you is with you.

LET HOPE INTERRUPT YOUR STORY

I once read on a painted sign hanging from chicken wire in a church kitchen that
"God don't make mistakes."
He don't.
He made you and you are not a mistake.
You've never been a mistake.
You and I have made mistakes, but we are not a mistake.

His soft and holy hands knitted you together as He sang a song of love.
He chose your shape and size and skin and soul.
He picked out your walk and talk.
He gave you weird and different, beauty and dreams.

He put a heart in your chest and life in your bones and stars in your eyes.
He filled you with love and tapped you on the nose and called you very good.

You.
He called *you* very good.

But I know you have days where you feel far from very
good. I feel that too.

There are days when I feel lost and alone, far from home.

There are days when the pressure builds beneath my skin
and anxiety shakes me like a hurricane rocks a house.

There are days when my past catches up to my present and
whispers in my ear
all the things I wish I had never done or said or thought or
heard.

And there are days when the heaviness tries to steal away
my hope,
pulls down the shades and blocks out the sun.
The darkness sits on my chest as I feel like
I am about to break and bend,
but hope says this is not the end.

Hope interrupts the story and shines a light,
reminding me that by God's grace
        everything will be alright.
After all, I have been knit together by His soft and holy hands.

Let hope interrupt your story.
Let hope slow you down as you stay awhile.
Slow down and stay awhile.

WHAT TODAY WILL BRING

Once again, the morning arrives with new mercies.
God takes His pointer finger and swirls the colors in the sky for us to see.
Slow down and stay awhile, I think He whispers.
I'm with you, I know He says.
It's as if God understands the day is about to groan loud.

Sides shout, fingers point.
To-do lists pile up and grocery prices rise.
Someone says something awful, and someone else says something worse.
Division works every angle to pull us apart.
Lies are told, truth is wrestled.
Noise fills our ears, weight rests on our chests.
Anger finds and fills our veins, anxiety sneaks in, all while hope fights back.
Hope is good at fighting back—even these days.

These days—
We wonder if everything will be okay.
We forget God tells us everything will be okay.
We forget what we want to remember and remember what we've tried to forget.

Distraction and destruction demand our attention,
and before we know it, we've wasted another day
    staring at screens.
We question almost everything,
    but God never questions if He loves us.

He does.

So—
We hold fast and continue to bless those who curse us and pray for those who hurt us.
We continue to confess our shortcomings and ask God for forgiveness.
We continue to turn up our hands and show the world all that God has given us.
We endure with mercy, hope, and love.
We try to put our phones down and look up to see the colors God has swirled in the sky.
We try to remember we can slow down and stay awhile with the One who is with us.
Because for all we do not know,
    we do know this:

God is with us.

READY TO LIVE

Something inside me cannot settle. I don't know what it is. Maybe I've been drinking too much coffee and not enough water. Maybe it's because I look at my phone more than the sky. Maybe it's because I'm stuck in the past and forget to be in the present.

Some days I feel like nothing's wrong, but something just isn't right. Some days I feel like a glass half full, but the wrong glass. Some days I feel like there isn't much more to the story, but I'm not even halfway through the book.

My head is a loud place that's always moving. It's a carnival ride, and I'm sick to my stomach.

When people ask me how I'm doing, I tell them I'm keeping busy. I used to believe that was the right answer, but these days I'm beginning to think it isn't. Maybe the way things are isn't the way they're supposed to be.

The other day I sat in my car before going into the grocery store. I was trying to find the energy and mental space to cross another thing off my to-do list. Sometimes life feels like one long to-do list. I sat in the quiet of my car, but somehow the quiet felt loud.

I watched an elderly man walk out of the grocery store. He loaded up his Jeep Cherokee and pushed his cart to the return spot. Then he gathered a couple of shopping carts scattered around the parking lot. He wasn't checking his phone or looking for someone to thank him. He just saw what needed to be done and did it. I watched him pick up a piece of trash and throw it away. He smiled at people as they walked out of the store. He waved to a little girl as she held her mother's hand, and she waved back. He stopped in the middle of what he was doing to watch a flock of birds fly above and away. He pointed to a plane, and the little girl looked up. She said, "Wow!" and they waved goodbye.

I WONDER WHEN HE DECIDED HE WAS READY TO LIVE.

I wonder when this man figured it out. I wonder if he ever felt how I feel. I wonder if he sat in his car one day and wondered if there was more to life than crossing things off a to-do list. I wonder if he watched someone older than him put shopping carts away and wave to children and stop to watch the birds fly above and away. I wonder when he decided he was ready to live.

Because I will remember exactly where I was when I decided.

GRIEF

Hold your grief for as long as you need.
Grief is not something to get over, but something to carry forward.
Grief brings a storm of change.
There is rain and thunder and stillness and lightning
and a rainbow,
and when you least expect it, a hurricane.

If you need, sit here with the silence or replay the memories
or gather close to the celebration.
Somehow there is joy in this too.
Maybe you've seen it or you're still looking for it.
Keep looking.
Honor the past with the time you have.
As you know, it's all fragile.
Don't listen to them when they say it's time to let go.
You don't have to let go.

Keep holding on to the beautiful memories and moments
that flood your mind and keep you awake at night.
You don't have to let go, but there will be a day when you begin to move forward.
Every step is a small step.

It's okay to move forward, to keep living.
Those you love may no longer be with you, but you are not without them.
Ahead you'll find steps forward and back, a heavy, aching heart, and glimmers of light.
Even on the darkest of days, there will be light.
Look for it. It will be there.
Sadness isn't something to be solved,
but a heaviness to be met with love.
Open your hands and let the light touch your grief.

I'M NOT SURE WHAT COMES NEXT

I'm not sure what comes next.

Maybe it will be good news, or maybe not-so-good news.
Maybe my prayers will be met with a yes
or with another season of waiting and wondering.

All I know is I have made it this far.
I have made it through the uncertain and the unknown
and the unexpected.
I have made it through surprises and struggles and storms.
I know that all this time God has been faithful and loving and kind.
Whatever comes next, God will continue to be faithful and loving and kind.

I guess what I am trying to say is I have made it through
what I never thought I would make it through,
and I am still here.

Maybe that's what I need to remember as I take
the next step:
I am still here, and I am still making it forward and through.

ENJOY IT

Enjoy it.
Those are two words my mind cannot let go of.

I am not charismatic, but I believe God placed them there.
Long ago He pulled back the dirt, planted the seeds,
gave them what they needed to grow,
and is now inviting me to rest with what has come to be.

To slow down.
To be where I am.
To give thanks.
To enjoy it.

God is good at giving us what we need,
and I think these two words are what
I've been longing to hear.

Enjoy it.

It's not a command, but an invitation.
Almost as if to say life is better this way.
But it's hard.

This morning I woke up feeling panicked.

It was like my heart and mind were playing tug-of-war and the victor was set to receive the winning prize of anxiety. Maybe it was because I broke my rule and scrolled through social media before falling asleep last night. Maybe it's because I haven't been able to write anything *good* for the last month or so. Maybe it's because my hair is falling out and I'm not ready to no longer be young. Maybe it's because I've gotten good at what I wish I was bad at: comparison.

When I start to spiral down the path of comparison,
I forget all this is a gift.
I forget I am not what I do.
I forget life is not a race.
I forget goodness and mercy.
I forget comparison is a trick.
I forget I can love this life and all that comes with it.
I forget I can accept God's kind invitation and enjoy it.

AT HOME IN GOD

Let yourself see you are at home in God. See the sun cast a shadow on the hardwood floor. Notice the plant in the corner bending to the east window. Smell the candle burning endlessly in the kitchen. Go to the fridge and see it fully stocked. Peek into the backyard and be amazed at the growing garden.

Here we have all we need.
Love and mercy, grace and joy.

God will not ask you to pay rent or tell you to leave.
He will say what He has said.
"Come, stay awhile."

YOU CAN SHARE YOUR STORY AND YOUR SCARS.

Sing and dance, bake and eat, rest and receive. You can ask your questions. You can share your story and your scars. You can find rest on the couch in the living room or on the front porch if you prefer.

Here, you'll change. You'll change the way you see the world and yourself and others. The way you see God will change too. Your shoulders will loosen and your load will lighten. You'll rediscover the spark that's always been in your eye. You'll find peace in the stillness and purpose in His presence.

And never again will you wonder where God is. He is at home. With you.

AS YOU WAIT

As you wait, make your coffee.
Move to the couch or to the chair on the porch.
Leave your phone in the other room, along with your worries.
You don't need to busy yourself.
You can just be.

Open your hands and breathe in deep.
This is a prayer of thanks and surrender.
Fix your eyes forward on the world in front of you.
See the trees shake their leaves to the ground.
Listen as the birds sing their song for anyone who will listen.
Get lost in the rising sun and the shadows it makes.

Slow yourself down and sit with what is, even if what is feels incomplete.
There is peace, but there is also a piece missing.
Something is missing, but hope is not.
Something is missing, but peace is not.
Something is missing, but God is not.
God is here as you wait.

SQUEEZE ME OUT

Squeeze me out.
And no, you won't find answers,
but maybe something softer,
something that stayed after the clapping stopped,
after the room emptied and the unexpected arrived.
I hope you'll find something like honey after the sting,
something gentle enough to hold you,
strong enough to stay.
Something patient, something kind.
Not loud, not polished, but real.
And mostly, I hope you find love.
Not the kind sold in songs,
the kind that wakes early just to water what isn't
  blooming yet.
The kind that daily pulls the weeds,
kneels in the mud, and calls it holy.
A love that whispers your name when you've lost your own
  voice.
A love that limps through dark valleys,
that forgives when it's tired,
that shows up again and again,
because that's what love does.

Press me; you'll find prayers whispered in silence,
tears that have seen the middle of the night,
faith that's been held together by the hands of a Healer.
You'll see joy that had to be chased,
hope that refused to let go,
and peace that passes all understanding.
Maybe you'll see unfinished dreams,
scars too honest to hide,
stories still being written by the same hands that held me together.
You'll find soul, grace, and the echo of every "I'm still here."
Squeeze me out, and no—
you won't find answers; you'll find presence.
No fear—just a heart still learning how to love and be loved.

COME BACK TO YOURSELF

Put down your phone, that lifeline-turned-leash.
Step outside, shoes off, bare feet on welcoming ground.
Let the grass preach peace to your skin.
Let the air touch your face
    like it's trying to tell you you're still alive.
You are.
Come back to yourself.
You've been somewhere else, haven't you?
Buried under lists, lost in endless headlines,
    suffocating under the pace of it all.

Let yourself breathe
    slower,
    slower still,
    and then slower again,
    because rushing won't resurrect you.

Drop the weight your shoulders are carrying.
It's heavy, isn't it?
This whole thing—
    living,
    waiting
    enduring,
    trying to hold it all together
    when you hardly know what "together" means anymore.

Silence the noise—
not just outside, but in.
Turn the volume down on the fear
        on the "what-ifs,"
        on the "not enoughs."
Cut through the static and listen.
Listen.
Do you hear it?
The birds, the wind,
the whisper in the leaves,
They're singing something ancient,
        something holy.
Creation hasn't forgotten how to worship.
Maybe we just forgot how to listen.
Remember:
Not your failure, not your fear.
But these:
faithfulness,
love,
forgiveness,
heaven,
the empty tomb,
grace upon grace upon grace.

Look around.
Goodness, right there beside you.
Mercy, moving in the margins.
Life is still happening, still unfolding,
even here, especially here.
So be still in the silence—
    not because you're stuck,
    but because stillness is sacred.

Inhale.
Exhale.
Repeat.

Speak like God is listening, because He is.
Listen like God is answering, because He is.
Be still like God is with you, because He is.

II

LEARNING & CHANGING

SHOW UP

Show up with your weaknesses
and your sins
and your questions.

God will show up with His strength
and His softness
and His love.

He always does and always will.

In this we can rest.

WHEN YOU DON'T KNOW WHAT YOU WANT

What do you do when you don't know what you want?

When all you know is that you don't know?

You're weighed down by waiting and paralyzed by what-ifs. There is fear and there is worry and there are a thousand outcomes for a thousand different decisions.

Comparison creeps and calls and keeps you from the beauty before you. Most days you're tired and feel like you're behind or running out of time. You watch the world move and hear what everyone wants for you, but you don't know what you want for yourself. You don't know about this or that, here or there. All you know is that you're alive, but you don't feel like you're living. Not yet. And that is what you want: *You want to live.*

You close your eyes and fold your hands to pray, but you don't have the words and are left wondering if everything is going to be okay. You tell yourself it will be, but you still feel far from whole. Life has become what you never thought it would be: unfulfilled dreams with a side of endless wondering. There is pressure to decide all the life things—

what to order for dinner,
how to respond to the email you've been putting off,
how to help your child navigate another new season,
what to watch while you scroll on your phone.

But deciding comes with the apprehension of choosing wrong, and the last thing you want is to be wrong.

You want to say something to God but know He speaks silence fluently. What a comfort it is to believe He knows what you're saying when you say nothing at all.

YOU LONG TO FEEL AT HOME IN THE WORLD.

You try to be still, but your mind keeps moving, always moving. You long to feel at home in the world. You hope for the right kind of change. You dream of feeling light and free.

You unfold your hands and cut the silence and ask God to help you let go of needing to know, to give you the courage to step into the unknown. With faith you ask God for something more than just okay, for something better.

And you don't know what that means, but it's as honest as you can be.

You know you want *something better.*

You want to *live* something better.

WHAT WAS I MADE FOR?

I was made for Monday mornings and Sunday nights and all the time in between. I was made for wonder and beauty. I was made to handle hard things with soft hands.

Like a strong tree I was made to endure seasons and to grow through them. I was made for grace upon grace. I was made to arrive and to go, to be welcomed and sent off. I was made for times of joy and grief and moments that hold both. I was made for confession and worship, heaviness and hope. I was made to hold still in the truth, to rest in the promise of a great Love.

I WAS MADE NOT BY ACCIDENT, BUT ON PURPOSE.

I was made to be who I was meant to be.

I was made to sit around the table with laughter and tears and cold drinks and homemade brownies and glimpses of a life and world to come. I was made for helping, for pulling back the dirt and nurturing life into this world. I was made not by accident but on purpose.

When you begin to wonder what you were made for, quiet yourself and softly say, "This."

KEEP BELIEVING

MAY I BEGIN TO SEE
THAT MY UNCERTAINTIES
AND QUESTIONS
ARE INVITATIONS
TO LIVE BY ~~SIGHT~~ FAITH
AND NOT BY SIGHT,
TO KEEP BELIEVING
THAT GOD
IS MAKING
ALL THINGS RIGHT.

YOU ARE BETTER

A Note to God

For a while, I thought You were frustrated with me.
As of late, I even thought You were disappointed
with every choice I've been making.
I thought my questions were annoying You, and my sins—
You know the ones I seem to always be confessing—
were pushing You further away.
Like I could have that much power.
For one reason or another, I began to believe the distance
and silence to be punishment.
Life felt like a time-out,
and I was waiting for You to say,
Okay. You can get back to living now.
I've told myself many things, and it seems only some of
what I've said has been true and kind.
My mind is best at believing the lies—
You know the ones that grow loud when life just isn't right,
when something doesn't feel right.
It's like taking a marker to a beautiful painting.
In my searching I added to what was already perfect
and holy.
Maybe it's because You are not who I want You to be.
While all along, You are still who You've always been.

Slow to anger.

Patient.

Loving.

Inviting.

Compassionate.

Merciful.

You are not who I want You to be; You are better.

NOT ALL GROWTH IS SEEN

When you believe something more is happening
than what you can see,
you'll be able to continue light and free.

You'll see you are not just floating through this life,
but you are living.
Feet on the ground, hands off the wheel.

You'll see hope in the heartbreak, magic in the mess,
purpose in the pause.

Through steps forward and back, stretches of fear and
unrest, you'll see how all things are working for good.

Yes, there will be pain and questions, stretch marks and
unwelcome situations.
There will be seasons of heaviness and unwanted
moments of misery.

You'll wonder if you've missed the turn. You haven't.
You aren't late, but on your way.
Just because the tree isn't getting taller doesn't mean the roots aren't stretching deeper.
Not all growth is seen.

When you cannot imagine how you'll get through what you're going through, keep going.
After all, something more is happening than you can see.

YOU'RE STILL HERE

Don't let yourself forget how you've made it to
    where you are.
All the prayers, all the steps.
All the pain, all the breaths.
May you always remember how far you've come,
how much you've grown,
and all God has done.

As you continue,
may you look back and see what led you to
    where you are.
The mountains and valleys.
The wins and failed attempts.
All the twists and turns in your story.

Through it all, you're still here,
God is still good,
and hope is alive.

YOGURT

The other morning, I opened the refrigerator to get yogurt and couldn't find it. I knew it was in there, but where? I searched and searched but could not locate it. I closed my eyes and opened them again as if the yogurt would magically appear.

No yogurt.

Then, desperate, I crouched down. Nothing. I shut the refrigerator door and opened it again. Still no yogurt. I walked to the other side of the kitchen and back. I got on my knees, I moved things around, I called out for it, I even prayed to God, and still no yogurt.

Finally, I asked my wife for help. She opened the refrigerator door, reached in, and pulled out the yogurt. It was right in front of me the entire time. In the center of the middle row. And I missed it.

GOODNESS IS NEAR.

Sometimes we need help seeing what we are looking for, especially when it is right in front of us. Sometimes the good is hard to find when the pain of the world is too much. Sometimes joy seems far when fear clouds our vision. Sometimes hope feels distant when life gets heavy.

But the other morning, when I was looking for yogurt, I was reminded that the good, the joyful, the hopeful are there. They may be hard to see amid uncertainty and chaos, through the cracks of pain and in the dark shadows, but I believe they are there.

Goodness is near. Joy is not distant. Hope is here. Keep looking. Ask for help if you cannot see. They're there.

BEFORE YOU GET AHEAD OF YOURSELF

Before you get ahead of yourself,
stop.
You do not need to let your thoughts run you away from yourself.
Open your hands and breathe in deep
and lean in as you speak truth over and into the noise in your head.
Say what Jesus said to the storm.
"Peace, be still."[1]
Remind yourself of what Jesus said during the Sermon on the Mount.
"Blessed are the merciful, for they will be shown mercy."[2]
Consider what Jesus said to the disciples.
"Let the little children come to me."[3]
And remember you are one of those little children.
You've always been, and you always will be.
Go to Jesus.
Before you get ahead of yourself, stop, and go to Him.

HARDER TO SEE

It's all getting harder to see.
The future, the past, and what is right in front of me.
Some days I feel like I am losing the person I used to be.
The person I wanted to become.
The person I am becoming.
But maybe clarity isn't required to continue forward.
Maybe I just need to hold on to hope and joy.
No matter how small they feel.
Maybe I need to go forward with faith.
Not knowing what is next.
But trusting I don't need to see to believe God is with me.

CHANGE IS COMING

Change is coming.
And yet, God remains the same.

Change is coming.
And yet, I am loved.

Change is coming.
And yet, God continues to give me His peace.

Change is coming.
And yet, every piece of me is here to be held.

Change is coming.
And yet, I know that where I am, God is too.

I AM STILL HAPPENING

There has been joy
and there has been grief.

There have been answers
and there have been questions.

There has been thankfulness
and there has been hurt.

For all that has happened
I am who I have become.

And I am still happening.

By all that has happened
I am still happening.

FRESH-SQUEEZED ORANGE JUICE

When I was five years old, my mom and I picked oranges from Papa's backyard. Just outside his front door were rows of orange trees that, to my young eyes, seemed to multiply into the horizon. Our grocery store plastic bags flapped in the Florida breeze as we walked the rows of orange trees, looking for the perfect place to begin. After a while, my arms became heavy with my half-full bag of oranges, and I asked the question all five-year-olds ask: "Are we done yet?"

"Not yet," Mom said from the next tree over. "We need enough to make fresh-squeezed orange juice in the morning!"

The very next morning, we stood in the kitchen and cut the oranges in half, squeezing them dry. We pressed them against the juicer and watched as the juice slowly drained into the bowl. My tiny hands struggled to wrangle the slippery oranges. I gritted my teeth and squeezed tightly as Mom encouraged me to "get every last drop." I made a mess, but she didn't mention it. I guess she knew messes were necessary to get something good.

My little hands grew tired, and I asked if we were done yet.

"Not yet. Good things take time."

We kept cutting and squeezing and cutting and squeezing.

When I got frustrated, she showed me how to keep my hands steady and strong.

When I tried to go fast, she gently reminded me to slow down.

GOOD THINGS TAKE TIME.

When we were finally done, we had two full glasses to show for our hard work. With the morning sunlight creeping through the blinds, we raised our glasses, and Mom said, "There is nothing better than fresh-squeezed orange juice."

We drank from our glasses until they were empty and dry.

When I was twelve years old, Mom and I once again picked a plastic bag full of oranges. The next morning, we cut them in half and squeezed them dry, just like we had years before. This time my hands were bigger, but I still made a mess, though less of one. Again, I tried to speed up the process and skip to the good part, but Mom kindly reminded me to slow down and not rush and keep my hands steady and strong as I squeezed.

We got every last drop, and when we were done, we drank from our glasses until they were empty and dry.

This morning I bought a bundle of oranges from the store. They were fresh, but not like the ones from Papa's backyard. I went home, cut them in half, and kept my adult hands steady and strong as I drained their juice. Again, I made a mess, but that only meant I was onto something good, because you cannot have something good without making a mess. Mom is a few hundred miles away, but she's right here in this kitchen with me, reminding me to slow down—reminding me how good things take time.

I can't help but think how all those mornings in her kitchen, she wasn't teaching me just how to start my day with fresh-squeezed orange juice; she was teaching me how to live. How to squeeze life dry. How to get everything it has to offer. How to make a mess, clean it up, and start again.

This morning I got every last drop from the oranges, filling two cups.

One for me and one for my mom.

LET CHANGE COME

Let change come.
I am made of it.
Shaped by seasons, aged by storms,
surprised by hope, overwhelmed by joy,
transformed by transitions, shattered by surprises.
I've sat in grief, been guided by grace.
I've said my goodbyes, heard the hellos.
I've witnessed light dissolve darkness, time heal wounds.
Water has washed over me
while words of life were spoken.
I've tasted.
I've seen.
I've endured.
I've changed.
I remain.
Let change come.

TRUST & BELIEVE

WHEN LIFE ISN'T
WHAT YOU THOUGHT
IT WOULD BE,
GIVE YOURSELF
A MOMENT TO SIT AND BREATHE,
AS YOU TRUST AND BELIEVE
SOMETHING MORE IS HAPPENING
THAN YOU CAN SEE.

KEEP TRUSTING

I'll keep trusting this is the direction God has asked me
to go.
And there are so many days I just do not know.
But He's taken me up and down mountains
and through forests and deserts.
He's heard my cries and understands why I am asking why.
I always feel like I am asking why.
He's gathered my worries and set them on fire with peace.
And for all I do not know—
and there is much I do not know—
I am beginning to see that it is in uncertainty that I grow.
So, I'll keep trusting.
Keep trusting.

WELCOME TODAY

Welcome today.
Welcome the mundane—
    because even the ordinary holds wonder.
Welcome the simple—
    because life is anything but.
Lean into now.

Not tomorrow, not someday—now.
Unclench your fists, turn your hands upward,
and take what God is offering.

Quiet mornings and early nights.
Laughter around the table.
Silence in the car, stuck in traffic but stuck together.
A message from an old friend.
A moment with a stranger who somehow feels like home.
An answered prayer.
The memory of a moment you'll never forget.
The scent of coffee brewing.
The sound of soft footsteps on the floor.
The memory of the one who has passed.
The colors of the morning sky.
The flowers that push through the spring,
reminding us that even the coldest winters pass.

Pause in the peace.
Let beauty break through.
Reach out, hold on—don't let go of today.
Because life happens in the moments we stop running,
stop reaching, stop waiting for something else.

Even if where you are isn't where you thought you'd be,
even if the road ahead looks nothing like the map you
drew—stay.
Stay in the story.
Stay in the mystery.
The hope we hold carries us through the fire.
The love we trust leads us through the storm.
The life we seek is found in the life we have been given.

GOD, I DON'T KNOW. AMEN.

"God, I don't know. Amen."

I've been saying this prayer for years, and I'm sure I'll be praying it for the rest of my life.
It's a prayer I am only beginning to understand.

It's a short prayer.
A simple prayer.
An honest prayer.

How does God respond to such a prayer? If we listen carefully, I think we always hear Him answer, saying something along the lines of:
Be not afraid or *I am with you.*

I'm learning that saying we don't know isn't a sign of weakness; it's a sign of trust and surrender.
With these simple words, I am asking for help, and asking for help has never been a sign of weakness, but of strength.

These days it's difficult to find the right words.
Between the uncertainty in my own life, the ongoing pain
of this world, and the constant news of hate and hurt, I
am often left speechless.
It's no different when it comes to prayer.
Some days my mouth is empty.
I give God my most honest exhale.
I open my hands and say, "Here."
I close my eyes and remind myself that Jesus has
died for my sins and the tomb is empty
and this is not the end.
In my silence I am reminded that
God makes sense of my groans,
and He knows what I say when I confess, "I don't know."
Because I don't know.
But He does.

How beautiful it is not to know, but to trust that He does.
He knows the reason behind our worries.
He knows the truth behind our questions that begin with
who, what, how, when, and *why.*

For all I do not know, I hold close to what I do:
In all that is heavy, there is hope.
Yesterday is over, today is here, and
tomorrow has yet to come.

ALL THIS TIME HAS NOT BEEN WASTED

ALL THIS TIME HAS NOT BEEN WASTED.
ALL THIS TIME YOU'VE BEEN BREATHING.
ALL THIS TIME YOU'VE BEEN GROWING.
ALL THIS TIME YOU'VE BEEN CONTINUING.
ALL THIS TIME HAS NOT BEEN WASTED.

IN THE STILLNESS

In the stillness
I will wait with hope
as beauty continues
to make itself known.

And when it arrives—
because beauty will arrive—
it might look different
than the way I painted it
inside my mind.

ONE SINGLE PANCAKE

"Do you know what you want?"

"Just one single pancake."

"One single pancake?"

"Yes."

"Blueberries? Chocolate chips?"

"Nope. Just the one single pancake, please."

"One single pancake it is."

"Thank you."

This was the first conversation I had today. I woke up craving a pancake and decided to go to a local diner to satisfy my need.

I sat alone at the bar and sipped on black coffee and read *The Inner Voice of Love* by Henri Nouwen as I waited for my pancake to arrive. Nouwen's words are honest and hopeful. Every page of the book seems to have something I need to hear and hold on to. Just as the waiter refilled my mug, I underlined these words: "Jesus is where you are, and you can trust that He will show you the next step."[4]

I faced the front door and the long line of recently washed windows. I watched as people parked their cars and dragged themselves through the front door. Humans look like zombies in the morning. Everyone is tired and trying and ready to say a two-word prayer to their server: "Coffee, please."

When I sit alone at restaurants, I let myself see the entire room. I'm curious and easily distracted and good at doing both. If people-watching were a sport, I'd have a lot of trophies. I've learned that when I sit with others, I need to have my back to the world so they can have my full attention. If we go to a restaurant that has TVs, you can kiss the conversation goodbye.

IF PEOPLE-WATCHING WERE A SPORT, I'D HAVE A LOT OF TROPHIES.

I watched as a silver Tesla parked three spaces from the front door. A man with a topknot got out first and then his wife and then their young son. The man and woman looked like they needed coffee and a nap. I wanted to tell them they were doing great, but if someone looks like they need coffee and a nap, then they don't need a conversation with a stranger.

On opposite sides of the restaurant sat pairs of men. Two at a table to my right. Two at a table to my left. One table was chatting about finances and business and stocks and blah blah blah. The other table was talking about the NBA playoffs. My ears perked up. If you start talking about NBA basketball near me, I am going to listen and, if appropriate, join your conversation.

The waiter brought my one single pancake with a smile and asked if I needed anything else. I didn't. I had all I needed.

TRUSTING IS TIRING WORK.

The restaurant began to fill up and so did I. Pancakes can find every empty space of your body and fill it full. When you eat a pancake, you feel joy, but soon that joy turns into drowsiness. No one has ever eaten a pancake and thought, *Now I have energy for the rest of the day.*

I continued reading my book, but I kept flipping back to those seventeen words: "Jesus is where you are, and you can trust that He will show you the next step."

Lately I've been thinking about trust. Life doesn't look the way I thought it would, and this has slowly sent me spiraling. Yet the invitation to trust Jesus remains. It always remains. Trusting is tiring work. It's as exhausting as it is beautiful. Yet, every day I find myself opening my hands and saying to God, "I trust You." Most days I even mean it.

Henri Nouwen was right: Jesus is present with us, and He will show us the next step.

Sometimes I have to sit in the corner and turn my back to the world to remember this is true. Sometimes I have to turn around and look back on my life and see how Jesus has been present with me, showing me the next step. Sometimes I have to go to a diner and order a pancake and sit in silence to let those seventeen words from page eighteen roll around in my head.

Jesus is where you are, and you can trust that He will show you the next step.

REACH OUT TO GOD

Reach out to God.
And then do it again.
Reach out with full or open hands.
Bring Him everything or nothing.
Show Him your scars and tell Him your stories.
Ask your questions and ask them again.

Reach out to God.
Put your hands in the air or tuck them in your pockets.
Write a letter or read what He's written to you.
Lift your eyes to the sky or close them tight.
Listen or scream or wait or sing.
Wonder out loud or inside your head.

He hears it all.
He has heard it all.
There isn't anything He hasn't heard, so say what you need to say.
You cannot offend God, but you can reach out to Him.
And maybe you'll see He has always been reaching out to you.

I AM BECOMING

I can feel myself becoming okay with what has come to be.
No, this isn't giving up.
And I'm not lying to myself.
This is becoming.

One prayer at a time.
One day at a time.
One honest sentence at a time.

I am unlearning what I should have never started to believe,
and I am beginning to believe the truth He has spoken
over me.
Like I am forgiven and chosen and loved.
I am giving up what was holding me down and giving back
what was keeping me from moving forward.

These days I am finding light in the darkness and hope in
the heaviness.
They have always been there, but sometimes it takes time
to see what has always been.
I am giving myself over to the hands of grace and resting in
the peace of His promises.
I am becoming okay with what has come to be.

YOU ARE NOT FASTER THAN YOUR FEELINGS

I woke up with fog on my brain and a darkness swarming in my soul.
This happens from time to time.
Depression doesn't check your calendar.
It spontaneously shows up whenever it wants and stays longer than it should.

The darkness was heavy, and the fog was blinding.
"When will you leave?" I asked.
No response.
Depression has selective hearing.
But I've learned how to get through to it.
I knew what I needed to do: *Lean in.*
You cannot outrun how you feel.
Believe me, I've tried.
You are not faster than your feelings.

I've learned I cannot sit at home with the pain.
I have to take it on an adventure.
So, off we went.
I threw on my favorite hoodie, grabbed the keys, and we drove to town.
Sometimes I drive in silence.
Sometimes I speak to God.

Today it was windows down with the music loud.
On days like this, you need to do things that help you keep going.
And what helps me when I begin to feel too much?

"One chocolate frosting donut with sprinkles, please," I said to the woman behind the counter.
"But, sir, you are a thirty-something-year-old man. Wouldn't you like something a little more manly? How about a maple bacon bourbon donut with gunpowder and tobacco?" is what the woman behind the counter didn't say.
That's what my brain said.

On days like this you have to be careful which voices you listen to.
The combination of fog and darkness will tell you things that are not true.
It's easy to believe the lies.
I woke up with them.
You're behind.
You're going to fail.
You'll never amount to anything.
Everyone is doing better than you.
It's not going to be okay.

Depression knows the perfect thing not to say but says it
anyway.

I grabbed the chocolate frosting donut with sprinkles and
walked down to the edge of the lake.
The sun decided to arrive, and it shone bright,
pushing the gray away, bringing the white clouds
from east to west.
Thank goodness the world didn't match my insides.
Thankfully today was not dark and foggy.

Keep finding the good, I told myself.
I stood alone and breathed in deep.
You're okay.
Sometimes you have to tell yourself what you need to hear.
You're okay.
Sometimes you have to tell yourself what you need to hear
again.

It's true. I am.
Life isn't perfect, but I am okay.

I am alive and free and standing beneath the sunshine on
the edge of the water with a chocolate frosting donut
with sprinkles.

I am okay.
And that's what I am leaning into.

DISCERNMENT

I was not made to keep up.
I was made with a different beat inside my chest.

I was not made to get ahead.
I was made to walk alongside others.

I was not made to shout.
I was made to listen for a still, small voice.

I was not made to always be on the move.
I was made for silence and rest.

I was not made for surface level.
I was made to go deeper, to see greater things beyond what
is in front of me.

I was not made for the noise.
I was made to be beside still waters.

I was not made for fame.
I was made for faithfulness.

I was not made to hold on and control.
I was made to let go and trust.

I was not made to hide.
I was made to be seen and known.

I was not made for there and then.
I was made for here and now.

I was not made for myself.
I was made to know God and walk with Him.

MAKE ME WHOLE

I don't remember when I began praying these three words, but I haven't been able to keep them from my mouth or out of God's ears for the last few years. Between moving to and from states, starting a business, watching my own insecurities and a long list of unanswered prayers keep growing, I began to crack and break. Each day brought new frustrations and complications. Life grew heavy. Most days I felt like I was trying to find the light switch in the middle of the night, running my hand up the bathroom wall in the dark as I tried to find my way forward.

I'd wake up earlier and earlier, which led to shadows beneath my eyes, showing a growing weight of heaviness and hopelessness. Unable to fall back asleep, I'd light up our dark bedroom with the dim light of news from social media. It was anything but peaceful, and peace was all I wanted.

News headlines told me how the world was ending. Facebook reminded me how death was out to get us all. Instagram decided it would be best to share skin care routines with me, and this is somehow by far the worst of the three.

The aching world seems to be groaning for wholeness, echoing the prayer I continue to pray: *Make me whole.*

With these three words, I am inviting God to remove the things that are keeping me away from Him, to tend to my aches and wounds and the things I cannot yet see or understand. I'm simply asking Him to help my hand find the light switch in the bathroom in the middle of the night, to help me find my way forward and through.

With these three words I am asking God to do what He does: *Draw near.*

Sometimes, especially in cold and low seasons, I need to remind myself of who I am praying to. Not a distant God who hears me only when I pray, but One who comes close to His creation. This is a God of love, justice, and mercy. He isn't afraid of my mess. He knows I just need a little help and a little light to keep going a little further.

MY CRACKS CAN REVEAL LIGHT.

As I've been praying for God to *make me whole,* I have started to see how my brokenness can be a blessing to others. My cracks can reveal light. My scattered and shattered pieces can become seeds that grow shade for others to find rest beneath.

God isn't blind to who we are or the troubles we face, but He leans in and points us to hope. He moves our hands to the light switch. He offers us peace, for He is ours. He sees our cracks and pieces and brokenness and gathers them in His hands and speaks to us: *Soon.*

Soon you will be made whole, and you will be with Me.

I have to believe God weeps with us. Just like Jesus wept when His friend Lazarus died. In our hurt, God does not turn away or hide Himself. He scoots His chair closer to ours. He places His fingers under our chins, lifting our heads to see what is before us. Peace Himself enters into what we wish did not exist. For if it matters to us, it matters to God. As we grieve and heal and continue, God is making us more like who He created us to be, not less.

Through it all, God is reminding us: Even in this, there is hope.

BUT TODAY, WHILE I AM HERE, I WILL CONTINUE TO LIVE WITH MY QUESTIONS AND DOUBTS AND CRACKS AND NAVIGATE THE UNEXPECTED.

The past few years have taught me that not much is going to make sense or feel right on this side of heaven. Prayers won't be answered the way I want them to be. Headlines will read of horrors and heartbreak. Phone calls will deliver knee-bending news. Friends and family members will breathe their last, and one day so will I. Grief and joy are around the corner. I just don't know which I'll face next.

But today, while I am here, I will continue to live with my questions and doubts and cracks and navigate the unexpected. As I go, I'll keep my eyes open for God's grace and mercy, for His peace and love. And at night, before I close my eyes, I'll open my hands and give to God what is weighing me down. I'll exhale the heaviness inside my chest and quiet myself in what I cannot help but believe: In Him all things are held together, and He is making all things new with love.

God is always doing more than I can see or give Him credit for. I'm sure that's something He and I will discuss one day over breakfast in paradise.

But for now, I'll keep running my hand up the bathroom wall and I'll continue to give God the broken pieces I carry around. And when I wake before the sun rises, I'll be quick to look up and ask with faith for God to make me whole, believing He will. Soon.

By grace, through faith, He will make me whole.

LOOK BACK

Look back and you'll see mountains and valleys and
footsteps that got you to where you stand.
You'll see changes and answered prayers and uncertainty
and pain and promise and something that will make you
want to turn around and walk the other way.
You'll see the answers to questions and questions to
answers and thoughts that fall somewhere in between.

Look back and you'll see a thread of grace God has woven
through what was and one you'll see when you look
ahead.
This grace is not to be abused, but it is free.
And you'll need it every step of the way.
Just like you'll need love.
And faith.
And community.
You'll need to be reminded you aren't done, but in many
ways you have just begun.

Look back when you need to, and move forward when you
are ready.
You are still here finding your way.
Ahead will be mountains and valleys and pain and joy.
You'll see God and He will see you.
You'll grow.
You always have been growing.
You'll change.
Just like you're changing now.
And at night when the stars arrive and the quiet finds you,
remember to exhale and look up.
You're right here, alive.
And He is with you as He has always been.

III

HOPING & BECOMING

REMINDERS FOR LIVING

You cannot live every life you want to live. You can live only the one precious life you have been given. This gift is more than enough. And once you realize that, then and only then can you live a deep adventure.

With this in mind, empty your hands and put down roots. The temptation is to leave home and live everywhere, but you can see the world without ripping up the soil you've been watering.

In this short life you are allowed to be right where you are supposed to be, so be all there.
Open your hands and ask God for daily bread and watch as He exceeds your every need.
Speak peace to every room you enter.
Hug a little bit longer and sing a little louder.
Grieve as deeply as you love and love as deeply as you grieve.
Keep trying and failing, but get back up and try again, this time softer.
Before you talk, listen and then wait.
This is a good way to pray too.
Be steady and faithful and dream beyond what you can see.

Leave fear far behind and cling to the goodness of mercy.
Always remember hope is not a trap and love is not a liar.
Take care of the earth and yourself and the people around you and let them take care of you.
You are not beyond help.
You are never beyond help.
Give grace, for you've been given an unending amount of it.
Trust you are loved regardless of what you do or what you have done.
Bless everything and everyone.
Look for God.
He is everywhere.

WHAT'S NEXT?

Lately a question has been rolling around my mind. I often find myself asking this question when I feel stuck or frustrated with where I am or, more recently, where I'm not. Uncertainty and insecurity fill my mind as I ask myself: *What's next?*

This question has become part of my prayers. Not at first, but eventually I look up and ask God. Sometimes I am slow to take things to Him, but I am learning. Sometimes I think I am a bother or a burden, but I'm not.

You aren't either. God is waiting and ready to listen.

What's next?

"GOD, I DON'T KNOW. AMEN."

I believe God knows, even when I don't, and I trust Him. Or I remind myself to trust Him when my mind begins to wonder and wander. For years I have been praying: *God, I don't know. Amen.* But these days I am starting to pray: *God, I don't know. But I know You know. You know. Amen.*

And He does. He knows.

I do not know what's next, but I do know God's love meets me where I am. I do not know what's next, but I do know all my needs will be met. I do not know what's next, but I do know there will be grace and hope and joy. I know everything will be okay.

How about that?

I guess I do know what's next.

WE WILL GET THERE WHEN WE GET THERE

Mom says, “We will get there when we get there.”
Which sounds like nothing but feels like everything.
This is just another way to say, “Don’t worry about it.”
Which is another way to say, “Trust God.”
Trust Him as you wait and pray and break bread and pour wine.
Trust Him as you do the dishes and water the bushes and sit in traffic.
Trust Him as you wonder about the future and look back on the past and sit with the present.
Trust Him as you count the days as they pass and the sheep as you try to fall asleep.
Trust Him as you weep and wait.
Trust Him as you stay and grow and as you go.
Trust God. We will get there when we get there.
Don’t worry about it.

PUT NINE DOLLARS OF GAS INTO YOUR HONDA ACCORD

When the noise inside your head gets loud and you feel yourself slipping away, scoot closer to the ones who say they love you. Return to your roots and put your hands in the dirt and grow with the seeds you plant.

Get off the couch and out of the glow of the TV and go binge-watch nature. Walk in the wilderness and sit by the campfire and look up at the stars. These are the same stars the disciples looked at after following Jesus all day only to sit side by side around a fire.

Put nine dollars of gas into your Honda Accord and drive around to the playlist you know inside and out, forward and backward. And then when you are ready, when you are miles down the road, shut off the noise and pray out loud.

FEEL YOURSELF COME ALIVE.

Tell God what you think. Every sentence is a song to God's ears. Play Him a concert. He never grows tired of hearing the music you make. Feel yourself come alive. Remember you were once dead, but now you are alive.

Remember the Holy Spirit lives inside you. Sure, your baptism was a long time ago, but what is time to God? To

Him a day is like a thousand years and a thousand years is like a day. Jesus invites you into the beauty of eternity now and a life empty of to-do lists and shame and middle school regrets.

Gather together. Let praise come from your mouth before you fill it with bread and wine. Clear the inbox and spam folders that take up space in the corners of your soul. Select the file folders of lies and fears you've collected and saved over the years. Drag and drop them into the trash. Create space to trust and be as you are, held by the truth He has spoken over you and me: You are loved.

LET YOURSELF BE MOVED BY THE LOVE OF CHRIST

Let the love of Christ wash you clean and make you whole
and keep you close to hope.
Let it empty your hands and fill your pockets.
Let the love of Christ spill over and into the lives of the
people around you.
Let it remind you that you are forgiven and free because
that's what love does.

Let the love of Christ give you confidence to step into the
unknown with faith.
Let it guide you through storms and valleys and Mondays
and decisions you don't want to make.
Let the love of Christ remind you of peace and goodness and
mercy and grace
and all the words you long to hear but have a hard time believing.

Let the love of Christ be your foundation, and may you build
upon it.
Let it lead you to sing and confess and trust.
Let the love of Christ give you ears to hear that nothing can
separate you from His love.
Let it bring you joy,
and may that joy slow you down to see the beauty that
surrounds you and me.

Let the love of Christ meet your grief and your sorrow and
your secrets.
Let it send you to places you never thought you would go
and into conversations you never thought you would have.
Let the love of Christ be your home.
Let it shine on those who need some light.

Let the love of Christ break down your walls and grow your
gardens.
Let it change you again and again and again.
Let the love of Christ point you to the truth,
and let the truth bring you to your knees as you look up,
give thanks, and say, "Amen."

AS YOU GO ON

MAY LOVE MAKE YOU BRAVE.
MAY GRACE MAKE YOU SOFT.
MAY FAITH MAKE YOU STEADFAST.

LEAVE YOUR HOUSE

Leave your house.

Roll the windows down and drive around town. Get lost in old mixtapes and playlists as you lose your voice and travel down new roads. It's good for you to get lost sometimes. Find a coffee shop and order an almond milk latte with honey and cinnamon. Life is short, so make it sweet. Sometimes you just need to spend seven dollars on yourself.

Leave your house and go to Costco.

You don't need to order your groceries directly to your front door. Go and be around people, even though you will get frustrated by how many people are at the grocery store. It's good for you to get frustrated sometimes. Get a case of sparkling water and enough boxes of macaroni and cheese to feed a small army. Before you get your receipt checked, buy a five-star dollar-fifty hot dog and smile at the greeter. You are not meant to be alone.

Leave your house and go to the park.

Leave your phone in the car. Walk the trails and notice the growing and changing world. You are growing and changing too. It's good for you to grow and change. Sit on the bench and watch your neighbors walk their dogs. Say hi to a stranger, but don't linger. No one likes a lingerer, but everyone likes to be seen and known. You are worth being seen and known.

Leave your house and go to church.

When the service begins, give thanks to God. He deserves all the praise. When it's time, share the peace of the Lord. Turn and shake hands and smile and be awkward. This is the only way to share the peace of the Lord. Put money in the offering plate. Sing off-key or out of tune, but sing. Nod during the announcements even if you aren't listening. You probably aren't listening. Stand for the reading of the gospel. Take notes or a nap during the message. Give thanks to God when the service ends. You are going with the peace of the Lord.

Make sure to leave your house. It's good for you.

WHAT I MEAN IS

When I say everything will be okay, what I mean is:
    In the end everything will be okay.
Along the way it will not all be okay.
You already know this.
There will be sadness and death and failure.
There will be brokenness and moments that feel beyond repair.
There will be pain and fear and unwanted changes to your story.
There will be seasons when you feel far from okay and moments when you wonder
    if the last line of this poem is true.
Of the little I know, one thing I know for sure:
    Through it all there is hope.
And hope invites us to lean in and hold fast to a light that continues to last.
It moves us to love and dream and give and continue and stay for another day.
It leads us to pray and forgive and cling to grace and believe the last line of this poem is true.
Everything will be okay, even if everything isn't okay today.

THERE WILL BE

There is much I do not know about tomorrow
or the next day,
about the world or my life or my future self,
but I do know there will be coffee in the morning.

There will be dogs at the park and love in her heart.
There will be stories and tears and moments that put a stitch in your side because you're laughing too hard.
There will be life and death and celebration and mourning.
There will be roads that end, others that begin,
and those under construction.

There will be charcuterie boards and dancing.
There will be sunrises and more stars than you can count in the sky.
There will be beauty and joy and hope.

There will be answers to go along with your questions and
questions to go along with your answers.
There will be dew on the grass in the morning and smoke
from the candles at night.
There will be self-discoveries and realizations and
complications.

There will be peace.
There will be miracles.
There will be grace.

And there will always be an invitation to begin again.

TOY TRUCKS AT CHURCH

He was maybe four years old. He had short blond hair and big brown eyes and was happy the way children are happy. He kneeled for most of the Sunday worship service as he pushed around his trucks on the seat of the pew, making soft sounds with his mouth. Some boys choose dinosaurs. Some choose animals. He chose trucks.

His older sisters were next to him, sandwiched between him and his mom and dad. My wife and I sat behind him, and every now and again he would look at me and smile before returning to his matchbox-sized trucks.

I imagine his mother said to him before they walked into church, "You can only bring three trucks this morning." Three is a holy number, after all. One was a yellow pickup truck. The other two were rigs without the trailers.

As we sang the opening hymn, he moved the trucks left and right, forward and backward. He was content, listening as he played. He bounced his head along to the tune as the wheels on the trucks went round and round. When it was time to pray, he parked his trucks and folded his hands and bowed his head and closed his eyes. As soon as we said "Amen," he went back to work.

When it was time for the children's message, he popped up from his knees and scooted past his sisters and parents before sitting next to our pastor. He listened and smiled and heard that we are God's treasure. We are precious and unique and worthy. We are found and cared for and loved.

WE ARE PRECIOUS AND UNIQUE AND WORTHY.

On the way back to the pew, he stopped and hugged his mom. He sat in her lap for a few minutes before crawling behind his sisters, returning to the end of the pew to play with his trucks. He continued to make soft noises with his mouth, powering the trucks gently across the red cushioned pew.

And that was the morning I learned worship is more than singing and praying.

YOU DON'T HAVE TO HAVE THE ANSWER

You don't have to have the answer
to take the next step.

You can just go.

And as you continue,
may you remember
the mountains and valleys
and the hope found in between.

May you hold close
the prayers and love
of those who are waving goodbye.

May you trust
His promises
and rest in His grace.

May you open
your heart, hands, and eyes
to the changing world around you.

You don't have to have the answer
to take the next step.

You can just go.

NEWNESS IS POSSIBLE

My hands are empty and tired and sore.
They've carried too much for too long, but not anymore.
Newness is possible.
It has always been possible, but I couldn't understand this with full hands.
I needed to let go to grow.
Letting go is worship.
It is painful and beautiful and holy.
It is looking in the mirror and standing in the presence of your enemies.
It is cutting off the crust of a peanut butter and jelly sandwich that isn't for you.
It is giving and receiving and growing and being.
It is taking a step back when you only want to take steps forward.
It is staying silent when you want to shout.
It is breathing in deep and confessing what needs to be confessed.
It is asking for grace and extending grace and receiving grace.
Newness is possible, but only with grace.

HOPE IS THE ONLY WAY HOME

If life rarely goes according to plan, then how do we live
knowing the life we want may never arrive?
We grab God by His hand and squeeze it.
We let our tears fall along with our questions, unafraid to
whisper, "This is not easy."
We loosen our grip on control, look to grace, and make our
home in the mercy of God.
We welcome the unknown with faith, trusting we've not
been forgotten.
We forgive, guarding our souls from the slow decay of
resentment, choosing—day after day—
to believe good is on the way, even when life feels
impossible or incomplete.
We place ourselves in the path of beauty and let it wreck us,
in the sacred and the small, in silence and in song,
in this life and in the joy of the next.
We measure life by the steady sacredness of ordinary days,
not by its highest peaks or lowest valleys,
not by our accolades or failures.
We meet our neighbors and strangers, our enemies, and
even ourselves with love.
We hold grief and heaviness with tenderness while
remaining ready to be surprised by kindness.

We learn to say "I don't know" with open hands, "help"
with humble hearts, and "I love you" without hesitation.
We live slow, knowing this is not forever, this too shall pass,
and one day we will dwell in the house of the Lord
forever.
We stand against injustice, walk against hate,
and move forward with grace,
step-by-step, side by side, hand in hand
with the One whose hand we squeeze,
the One we never let go of, the One who carries us through.
And although the questions and pain remain,
we continue to hope.
Because hope is the only way home.

HOLD STILL

Before you move on, hold still.
I know there is much to do and a world waiting for you,
but for a moment, let yourself be.
Let stillness interrupt your busyness as you create space to breathe.

For all you have to do, take a moment to hold still and remember.
Remember you were not created to always be doing and moving.
Remember mercy and grace and that all this is from God.
Remember what He has carried you through and that
you have a story worth living, a story worth sharing.

Remember Jesus meets you where you are
and where you are is right where you need to be.
Remember you do not have to have
all the answers to live today with faith and love.
Remember that despite your past you are forgiven and free
and sent to be a light for the world to see.

Let this be another moment that reminds you
of the One who has taken your sins away,
assures you everything will be okay,
and has made a way for you to live with hope day after day.
So, before you move on, hold still and remember.

IF YOU WANT TO CHANGE THE WORLD

If you want to change the world,
    get your hands ready.
Pull back the dirt, plant some seeds, and watch them grow.
Fold your hands and pray for all the things your
    heart and mind carry.
Open your hands and give what you have.
Tuck your hands in your pockets and listen.
Lift your hands to the sky and give thanks.

SLOW WORK

In this, continue to believe God is doing a slow work in you.
There is no need to fast-forward through today to get to
tomorrow quicker.
Today is the gift you have.

Keep yourself from skipping ahead to the good part,
and let yourself believe this is the good part.
In this, be still.
Trust that what God has started He will complete.

You aren't being led to the edge of nothing, but you're
slowly being guided
toward something beyond your imagination.
Give yourself time to unfold and bloom and be pruned back
again.

You are not behind, you are growing.
God is doing a slow work in you.
What He has started He will complete.

MOVING FORWARD SLOWLY

MOVING FORWARD SLOWLY
IS STILL MOVING FORWARD.
ANOTHER DAY.
ANOTHER STEP.
ANOTHER PRAYER.
ANOTHER BREATH.

KEEP MOVING FORWARD SLOWLY.

CARVE OUT YOUR CORNER IN THIS WORLD

I don't know what to tell you or what it is you need to hear. It seems as though everything has already been said and said again, and the last thing I want to do is weigh the world down with noise.

Everywhere you look someone is telling you something or your phone is buzzing with breaking news. It's probably buzzing now.

I don't know what you need to hear, but maybe you need to hear what I need to hear . . .

Carve out your corner of this world. Dig deep and wide.
Plant a garden and put down roots.
Stain your pants and get dirt beneath your fingernails as you come alive.
Be brave and kind as you become the person you needed when you were younger.
Pray something honest and pray it again.
Try a new recipe or eat the same cheese quesadilla you've been perfecting for years.
Then feed yourself with morning walks and sunsets and reminders of joy.
Listen and forgive and ask for help and, if you need it, a side of ranch.

Turn off your notifications and live today with more peace
than yesterday.
Follow hope instead of your heart.
Give yourself time to rest and breathe and remember living
doesn't always mean doing.
Stay inspired and ready to receive what you didn't see
coming,
because something good is always on the way.
Let your hair grow gray and write poetry
and say yes to the thing you've been wanting to say yes to.
Find what keeps you going, even if you walk with a limp,
and show the world what you're capable of.
Show up and give what you have and give it again and again.
Send that text and take that nap and journal about the wild
life you've been given.
Let your puns be intended and your compliments be
sincere.
Start a family or backpack across Europe or both. There is
time for both.
Don't believe the lie that there is not enough time to live
your life.
Carve out your corner of the world.
But do it all with love.

AS YOU HOLD WHAT HAS BECOME

When you turn around and see what has come to be,
I hope you give yourself some grace
as you hold what has become.

You found a way to make it through
and to another day.

You pushed and fell your way forward,
tripped and stumbled, got turned around,
mixed up, lost, and found.
You tested your faith while being carried every step of the way.

You were carried every step of the way.

Through the change and trying, and the seasons of trying to change,
here you remain.
Push back if you want, but you are loved all the same.

You've got pockets full of unanswered prayers
    and prayers answered in ways you never saw coming.
You've made it through,
    fight after fight,
    night after night,
    and you have been welcomed again and again
    by the gracious morning light.

You've grown and gone on, returned and been wrong.
You've wished and wondered and waited for this and that
  and the other.
You've searched and fought, been found and lost in thought.
You've tried not to lose your mind or believe the lie that you
  are behind.

Before you go on, hold what has been handed to you:

The broken and beautiful.
The sorrow and joy.
The heaviness and heartbreak.
The miracles and mysteries.

And as another new beginning arrives, open your hands
and breathe.
Turn around and see that goodness will continue to follow
you and me.
I hope you give yourself some grace as you hold what has
become.

YOU CAN JUST BE

When you have nothing more to give,
take a moment,
light the fire,
and watch darkness
be overcome by light.

See shadows slowly disappear,
uncovering the truth
that has always been
right in front of you.

Let the light remind you
that you do not have to be
everything for everyone.

Because the truth is
you can rest
and slow down
and let go
and be.

What a beautiful thing it is
to remember
you were created to rest
and slow down
and let go
and be.

You can just be.

LIVE TODAY

I want to live today.
Not yesterday or tomorrow, but today.
Extra cream cheese on my toasted everything bagel.
Another half mile on my morning walk as the sun climbs over the trees.
A long conversation with God and some small talk with my neighbors.
Screen time down, self-control up.
Brave and calm with low blood pressure.
Slow and kind like the voice of my grandmother.
That's how I want to live today.

ONE DAY

One day, I hope you forget about the thing that has kept you
wide awake and wondering.
I hope you find rest and peace.
Slowly, I hope you begin to see how God's timing is a
kind gift.

One day, I hope you look back and say *thank you* and *amen*
and *hallelujah* and all the other things your grandma
would shout or whisper during the Sunday sermon.
And I hope you say it like you mean it.

I hope you experience a miracle and don't brush it off as a
coincidence.
I hope you go through life clinging to the unending grace
that has been given to you.
I hope you never lose sight of heaven or the hurting or
of hope.

One day, I hope you find time to put your hands in the earth
and water and wait and watch as the
strawberries and blueberries grow and grow and grow.
And I hope you remember you were made to grow too.
To soak in the sun and become full of life.

HE IS HERE

WHEN I SLOW DOWN
AND LOOK AROUND
I BEGIN TO SEE
WHAT MY HEART
HAS COME TO BELIEVE:
GOD IS NOT DISTANT,
HE IS HERE.

WRITING DROUGHT

I am in a writing drought. This doesn't mean I don't have anything to say, but it means I don't know how to say what I'd like to say.

I don't know how to tell you that I saw the *Barbie* movie. I don't know how to tell you about the Chinese food I ate and how my fortune cookie read: "You will attract cultured and artistic people." I don't know how to tell you how I wanted to be with my mom in Florida for her birthday and not just celebrate her over FaceTime. Or that I miss my family and Florida and the way things were when I was four.

I don't know how to tell you about the breakfast I had the other day with my friend Ryan at a small-town diner. He ordered an omelet. Sausage, peppers, onions, and cheddar cheese with toast. I had two scrambled eggs, a pancake, and crispy bacon. My mom taught me to order bacon crispy. It's the right way to order bacon. Ryan and I talked about life and God and writing. We both had diner coffee, and I had a little too much, but somehow not enough. I was jittery for the next few hours, which kept me in my ongoing writing drought. But I kept in mind his writing advice: "Pay attention and write what you've got." So here I am, writing what I've got.

I don't know how to tell you about the teenage girl and teenage boy I see at church every Sunday. He looks at her more than the bulletin in his hands. She is always moving her hair behind her ear as she glances at him. They are the only ones in God's house who cannot wait until the part of the service when we share the peace of the Lord. Before worship begins, he will quietly whisper to her from three rows away, but last week he was only one row away from her. They don't know this, but when we get to the part of the service where we offer up prayers, I pray for them. "Lord, be with the boy in the blue shirt and the girl in the red dress as they fall in love. Let it be awkward and beautiful. May you give him the courage to sit in the same row as her next Sunday. Amen."

I don't know how to tell you about the two women I sat between on a plane a few weeks ago. How the woman to my right listened to a John Grisham book from her ten-year-old computer. How the woman to my left read a romance novel on her Kindle a little too slowly. How the woman to my right sneezed and dropped her phone beneath her seat. How the woman to my left had to get up from her seat so I could lie on the floor to grab the other woman's phone. How the woman on my left said to me "Wow, you're so flexible" in a way that made me uncomfortable. How the woman to my right said, "Sorry I made you do that," but I didn't mind.

I don't know how to tell you that on my next flight I noticed a woman who was about to lose her plane tickets. They were sticking out of her back pocket. When she stood up, they were waving right in my face. I tapped her on the shoulder and said, "Excuse me, ma'am, but I think you're about to lose your tickets." How she thanked me and thanked me and thanked me and thanked me and then told me, "Something good will happen to you soon. Karma." I smiled and nodded. I didn't know what to do with what she told me, so I just kept moving forward. And I'm still moving forward.

AND I'M STILL MOVING FORWARD.

I don't know how to tell you I'm still waiting for something good to happen to me. Or that this summer has been hard. I don't know how to tell you about a recent death and a recent tragedy and a recent email. Or about the conversations that have broken my healing heart. Or about our adoption process. I don't know how to tell you that waiting to become parents is emotionally draining. Or that I am still hopeful and still trusting. Or that I need a vacation. I don't know how to tell you I feel behind in life. Or that I've started to feel less like myself and more like someone else. Or that I am struggling to believe everything will be okay.

And I don't know how to tell you about the sky tonight. It is beautiful. No words can describe it. And that's a good thing, because I am in a writing drought.

THE SECRET TO LIVING

I have found the secret to living a full life.
It begins with slowing down
        and breathing deep
        and giving thanks.
And it involves pulling another chair to the table
        and remembering hope remains
        and saying yes to another slice of cake.

STAY CLOSE

Stay close to those who remind you who you are when you forget.
Because you will forget.
You'll need to be reminded
you are seen and loved and wanted.
You'll need to hear you are wrong when you are wrong,
just like you'll need to hear you are forgiven,
because you are.
You'll need to be reminded you are more than your past and hope is calling you into another tomorrow.
Stay close.
The truth is far too beautiful and heavy to carry alone.

LET YOUR FRIENDS BECOME YOUR FAMILY

Invite them over for Christmas Day, New Year's Eve,
and Wednesday evenings to watch *Survivor.*
Hang photos of them on your wall.
Put their children's artwork on your fridge.
Eat leftovers together.
Sit with them at church.
Pray with them and for them.
Pour champagne and raise a glass to what God has done.
Weep with them.
Ask questions.
Be curious, go deep, and keep going.
Let it all be done with love and let it all be done together.
Protect their names when they are not around.
Be one another's emergency contacts.
Create memories and moments you'll remember
even when you're older and have a hard time remembering.
Remind each other of grace.
Go through it together.
Whatever it is.
Say I love you.
Let faith, compassion, and hope be your foundation.
Make space for one another to be seen, heard, and
celebrated.

Name your group chat "Framily."

Tell their children about Jesus and what life was like before they arrived.

Believe them when they say, "You are family."

You are family.

Make yourselves at home in their home.

Know where they keep the silverware and peanut butter and extra toilet paper.

Water their plants when they are out of town.

Walk their dog.

Go to their mother's funeral.

Take their father's garbage down to the road.

Hug their brothers and their sisters like they are your brothers and sisters.

Remember, you are family.

As you get through what you're going through, make your friends your family.

A FEW REMINDERS FOR TODAY

Slow down and see the beauty beginning to grow from the
uncertainty.
Lean in and feel the freedom of grace upon grace upon grace.
Hold fast to the joy of another sunrise and sunset and the
light found between.
Receive with love the invitation to continue again and again.

WHAT I KNOW HOW TO DO

Today I'll do what I know how to do.
I'll make coffee.
I'll walk the dog.
I'll say a prayer in the morning
    and at night
    and throughout the day.
I'll wash the dishes after supper.
I'll watch the sunset slowly fade behind the trees.
And this, another day, will be holy
    and faithful
    and honoring.
I'll do the same small things with all the love I have
    because small things with great love matter.

With love, it all matters.

JOY

One day you will realize joy is not a full bank account.
It is not endless freedom or getting everything you want.
Joy is a full table.
It is the text that comes at the right time.
Joy is the sun rising and setting and being awake and alive
to see both.
It is hearing you are loved and forgiven.
Joy is receiving the body and blood of Christ.
Joy is needing a vacation from your vacation.
Joy is letting go and beginning again with grace.
Joy is all the little things that aren't really the little things.
It is watching the sky do its thing: lightning, shooting stars,
rain clouds, and fireworks.
It is smiling at a stranger and the stranger smiling back,
and for a moment you forget about all the things you've
been trying to forget.
Joy is a poem that puts into words what you are feeling.
Joy is opening your empty hands and knowing you have all
you need.
Joy has been set before you.
Pull up a seat and enjoy.

AT THE END

WHEN YOU FIND YOURSELF
AT THE END,
LOOK BACK,
GIVE THANKS,
AND WITH GRACE
BEGIN AGAIN.

DO NOT LET THE LITTLE THINGS GO UNNOTICED

Do not let the little things go unnoticed.
Look for them.
Slow down to see the way the clouds move and how the birds fly.
Notice the blooming flowers and the leaves as they change and fall and spin from the tree.
Watch the sky fade before the stars begin to shine.
Listen for the laughter in the distance and the dreams being whispered and sung in your soul.
Hold the world with your bare hands and be amazed
by the little, beautiful things God gives and gives again.

THIS IS NOT THE END

This is not the end. You're just learning how to begin again.
But there are some things you need to unlearn before you take another next step.
There are some cobwebs and spiders to clear and to kill.
There are lights to turn on and weeds to pull and seeds to plant.
There are wounds to kiss and lies to meet with truth.

You are not the only one who feels the way you do.
You are not the only one who feels like you are behind or running out of time.
You are not the only one who feels lost or uncertain.
You are not the only one who wants time to slow down or speed up or turn back.
You are not the only one who is praying for change or who has no idea what's going on.
You are not the only one who needs to hear you are loved and forgiven and worthy.
You are not the only one trying to find the courage to take the next step.
But you don't have to have the answer to take the next step.

Life is not something you can win, but something you can enjoy.
You can slow down and look around and remember all this is a gift.
Here, you will hurt and hope.
You will lose and love.
You will start and end and get lost and try again.
And you, no matter how hard it is to believe, will be okay.
You will be okay.

So, before you move on to the next thing, pause.
Sit with what is.
Just for a moment.
Open your hands and let go of what you're holding tight.
Breathe deep and exhale the heaviness that's been trapped inside.
Before you move on, find yourself in these words:
Life is not a race, and you are not behind.

GO ON

Adapted from my book *Walk a Little Slower: A Collection of Poems and Other Words*

Go on.

Wake up early.
Say a prayer.
Make your usual cup of black coffee.
Put a piece of bread in the toaster.
Toast it until it's golden brown and not a second earlier.
I know, it's hard to wait.
But wait.
It's almost ready.
Smear Land O'Lakes butter across the top and don't be stingy.
Life is too short to be stingy.
Forget your phone.
You don't need it to thank God.
You don't need it to sip coffee.
You don't need it to enjoy the last, buttery bite of toast.
It's a perfect bite.

Say amen.

Touch your toes.
Or try.
Or tell them you'll get them in heaven.
Go for a walk.
If you want, do the same walk you did yesterday.
As you go, walk a little slower.
Wave to the children.
Pick up the trash.
Wave to a neighbor.
Smile.
Always remember to smile.
Don't be creepy,
but smile.

Look up at the sky.
It's still there.
It was there yesterday too.
Did you see it?
God made the sky.
God made the clouds.
God made the birds.
You can wave to them too.

Do you see the trees?
They're changing and changing and changing.
Just like you.
Season after season.
Growing through the storms, swaying in the sunlight.
Look at the trees and remember how they came to be.
Like your faith, it all started with a little seed.
Remember how beautiful it is to believe.

And at night, step outside one last time.
Watch the sun fall into the silence of the horizon.
A daily reminder—
we were made to rest and rise and repeat.
Rest. Rise. Repeat.
Feel the light of the setting sun dance on your skin.

You're alive.
You're covered in grace.
You're seen.
You're significant.

From your head to the toes you cannot touch.
From your insides where the coffee mixes with golden
brown toast to your outside
where the light hugs your skin like an old friend saying
hello.
From your waking to your sleeping.
From your wondering to your realizing.
From season to season.
From your first breath to your last.
You're significant.

Go on.

YOU CANNOT GO BACK TO YOUR OLD LIFE

You cannot go back to your old life, and this is a good thing
    because it no longer fits.
Yesterday is a T-shirt that shrunk in the dryer,
        a life lesson turned hand-me-down
        for someone else's future tomorrow.

What I have come to know is that it's hard to hold
        what today is handing you if you're
        still holding on to yesterday.

You must let it go.

If discomfort is a sign of change, then we can expect
growing pains to come with becoming.
And through the stretching and testing,
        I've learned nothing is wasted.

I never would have grown if it wasn't for what has been,
        the mercy, the pain, the wonder, the long nights,
        the frustration, the wrestling, the waiting, the morning
                light.
Nothing is wasted.

I cannot be who I was, just like today cannot be yesterday.
But who I was made me who I am.

So here's to letting the past rest in peace and welcoming
today with grace.
Here's to continuing to change with the change, knowing
what's ahead is worth the letting go.
Here's to moving forward with eyes open wide, trusting
that God is a God of surprise.

What is won't last, and you'll begin to see how brave it is to
leave behind what was meant
to stay in the past.

Soon you'll begin to see how it is brave to leave behind
what was meant to stay in the past.

THIS IS THE GIFT

After all the waiting, the wondering, the winding roads—
here you are.
Take a breath; look back for a moment.

You've watched dreams take flight
and released things you thought you'd hold forever.
You've held tight through storms you didn't see coming,
and somehow, you've kept going—reshaped, but never ruined.
The days have folded into each other, and slowly, gently,
you've become someone new.
You have made sacrifices and enemies and tacos and friends and messes you are still trying to clean up.
You've got scars like scripture—true stories etched deep into skin and soul.
Some mornings you hardly recognize who you see in the mirror.
Other days you stand on top of the tallest mountain and shout, "This is me!"
There are lines like gutters on your face and your hands,
chipped and cracked, swollen and sore, but like your heart it will continue to give a little more.

You have seen better days and there are still better days to
be seen.

There are seasons when you slow down, and quietly
wonder, "Is this really it?"
All the tasks and to-do lists and heartbreaks and questions
and memories added up.
The red traffic lights. The bathroom breaks. The
appointments. The opening and closing of the
refrigerator door because you didn't know if you were
hungry or bored or both or neither.
But with the little light that is shining straight to you, I
hope you see just how precious life is.

This is the gift you have been given and
it's beautiful in the way only real things are:
imperfect, simple, more than you expected.
Open your hands; there's still more to receive—
more to give, more light to walk in.

There is still more.
This is the gift.

ACKNOWLEDGMENTS

First, it is important for me to thank God for coffee, dogs, and sunshine. Without those big three, this book would never have been written and life would be less enjoyable.

This book wouldn't have happened without Jonathan Merritt, who graciously said yes to being my literary agent. Thank you for putting up with all my ideas and for helping me take the next right step in my writing career. You have changed my life for the better, and my family and I will forever be grateful for you. I hope you get a nice vacation.

To the entire team at Zondervan/HarperCollins—especially Kara Mannix, Bonnie Honeycutt, Stephanie Newton, Kristi Smith, Amy Kerr, Chasity Edwards, and Tiffany Forrester—it is such an honor to have released this book with you. Thank you for your patience, grace, and encouragement. I hope you also get a nice vacation.

This book wouldn't have happened without my friends and their families. I'm hesitant to start listing names because I know I'm going to forget someone. Truly, the last thing I want to do is hurt or offend. So, if I forgot you, maybe you should have texted me more.

Gabe Kasper, Ted Doering, Matt Popovits, Ryan Tinetti, David Zahl, Phil Klopke, Tom Eggebrecht, Heidi Goehmann, Kyle Frazier, Marcus Lane, Shelly Schwalm,

Kris Stack, James Saleska, Gary Hickey, Matt Hammitt, Rachel Wheatley, Zachariah Thompson, Bill Yonker, Chip May, Kyle Willkom, Blake Roberts, Carter Hamric, Heather and Luke Mroczenski, Leah Abel, Jared Coad, Kimberly Phinney, Abbie Snow, Cody Case, Dave Connis, Jeff Cloeter, Bryan Moore, Seth Gehrke, Sarah Salzberg, Todd Nesloney, Rebekah Spaulding, Joe Souter, Andrew Milam, Taylor Jarman, Kayla Craig, Justin McRoberts, Ben Squires, Diamond Dogs, A-Team, Man Village.

To the College Community Group who willingly comes to our tiny little house every Thursday night: Y'all are truly the best of the best. It is a joy for Sarah and me to watch who you are becoming and to learn from you along the way. Keep it super cool, super chill, super hang.

To the Nashville Crew: Gosh. I love you all. You have walked with us through the best and worst. I don't know what else to say except your friendship has been life-changing, and I am so grateful for each of you.

Thank you to all the churches, conferences, organizations, schools, and coffee shops that have invited me to speak and share poetry with your communities. Your kind invitations and loving encouragement have given me the confidence to believe poetry is a worthwhile pursuit. I look forward to sharing many of the poems in this book with you in person soon.

Most of this book was written while in Arcadia, Michigan. I am forever grateful for the Camp Arcadia community. Even though you love Sarah more than me (look, I get it), your support and kindness have changed me for the better.

To the online community who has gathered around my words: Thank you for helping turn this dream into a career. Extra thanks to my Substack and Patreon subscribers, because without your generous support over the last few years, I would have certainly had to get a different job, one that probably would require wearing a tie and saying things like "I got your Slack message and I'll circle back after I crunch the numbers." That would have been very hard for me, mostly because I don't know how to crunch numbers, and this book would never have been written.

Adam Fricke and Justin Fricke. Remember back in 2000-something when I first started writing poetry? You've been with me through every step and season. Thanks for your continued support of this dream. Also, remember that one time we spent Thanksgiving eating Chinese food at a gas station? Go Magic.

Barrett Grebing. Back in 2018 we chatted on a picnic table outside of Red Horn Coffee in Cedar Park, Texas. That conversation changed my life. Thank you for not just believing in me but for helping me see what I couldn't. And thank you for always pointing me to Jesus. I owe you.

Blake Flattley and Matt Doering. It is a joy to share the stage with you all over the country. Your talent, heart, and friendship make every event not just a show but a shared story. Let's keep it rolling.

Trevor Kunze. To be your chosen brother is an honor. God knew what he was doing when he introduced us in 2009 at Camp Luther. Also, remember that one time we got lost in Germany? And the goats? Wild.

Aaron, Jane, Nolitha, and Micah. "Framily" was written for you because you are our framily. Always and forever. I do believe it is time to rum it back.

To Jan, Bruce, Marc, Cheryl, Jacob, Mikayla, David, and Talia: What a joy it is to be part of your family. Thank you for your generous support and loving-kindness.

To Tyler, Greta, Ethan, and Caleb: Thank you for your constant support and care. I hope this book reflects even a fraction of the love and inspiration you've given me. Love y'all.

To Mom and Dad: This is all your fault. You never told me to stop pursuing this dream of being a writer, even when it seemed insane. Thank you for not telling me to be realistic, because I probably wouldn't have listened. I love being your son. God knew what He was doing when He chose you to be my parents. I'll send you my Wordle and Sports Connections score in the morning. I love you.

Pancake. Because you're a dog, you'll never know that I wrote a book or that you were thanked in the acknowledgments. But without you, this book wouldn't have been written. You kicked me out of bed, took me on walks, and sat at my feet while I put this book together. It's just too bad you don't know how to read.

Judah. Getting to be your dad is the joy of my life. As I write this, you are eighteen months old. You are full of wonder and joy and curiosity and hope. I pray you always will be. And may you always know that I love you.

Sarah. I still cannot believe you said yes to marrying me even after I told you I wanted to be a full-time author and poet. Thank you for saying yes. You cannot take it back now. It's too late. Thank you for walking with me through the grief and goodness. What a life. And here we are, alive. How good and faithful God is to us. I love you, buddy. Always. Now, can we go visit Europe?

All glory to God.

NOTES

Part I: Getting Through & Going Through

1. Shelly Schwalm, conversation with the author, July 2023, Arcadia, Michigan. Printed with permission.

Part II: Learning & Changing

1. Mark 4:39 KJV
2. Matthew 5:7 NIV
3. Matthew 19:14 NIV
4. Henri Nouwen, *The Inner Voice of Love: A Journey Through Anguish to Freedom* (Image, 1999), 18.

ABOUT THE AUTHOR

TANNER OLSON is an author, poet, and speaker. He regularly shares his spoken word poetry and tells stories of grace and hope in churches and venues all across the country. His work has been described as "hopefully unique and inviting" as it blends faith, humor, and curiosity. Tanner is the author of four books, including his newly released first book for kids, *All the Things I Say to God*. He doesn't take himself too seriously, drinks his coffee black, and cheers for the Orlando Magic. He lives in Nashville, Tennessee, with his wife, Sarah, their son, Judah, and their dog, Pancake.

More from author Tanner Olson for the little readers in your life

All the Things I Say to God inspires children to connect deeply with their faith, discover the joy and simplicity of prayer, and experience the comforting love and presence of God in their lives. Find a copy today at your nearest retailer.